learn to SKI at home
in your stocking feet!

by

Larry 'Wild' Wrice

ISBN: 1492128465
ISBN-13: 9781492128465

THIS BOOK IS FOR BEGINNERS

AND FOR EVERYONE

WHO WANTED TO SKI BUT SAID:

"No, it's not for me"

OR

"I'm too old"

OR

"I don't want to break my legs"

OR

"I can't do it"

OR

" I tried but I couldn't understand my instructor"

THIS BOOK IS FOR YOU !

ADVANTAGES OF THIS BOOK ARE:

1. You can learn from an expert instructor with over fifty years experience.

2. This book will prepare you with everything you need to know for your first trip to the slopes

3. You can learn to ski in your stocking feet! You can learn in the comfort of your home or office. No snow or cold weather to learn in.

4. This is PRIVATE learning. No embarrassment from falling down in front of other people. You can surprise your friends!

5. NO expensive lessons, NO appointments to make, NO contracts to sign.

6. Take your time and learn at your own pace .

7. This method lessens the fear of skiing and adds an extra sense of security on your first day of skiing.

8. If you do decide later, to take lessons, you can be ahead of others in your ski class

9. BEST OF ALL! No expensive equipment to buy – you need only three easy to find articles that are often already in your home

EQUIPMENT REQUIRED:

1. TWO CHAIRS

2. BROOM OR MOP HANDLE

3. SMOOTH 4 X 4 FLOOR SURFACE

    (such as smooth carpet or a linoleum floor)

HERE I AM TEACHING AT
THE PLAYBOY SKI RESORT IN 1973!

CHICAGO DAILY DEFENDER—FEB. 3, 1973

Dry run first, now girls...

Associate ski instructor Larry Wrice (left) gives a group of beginners a few lessons in the new GLM method of skiing at the Playboy ski resort. The popular black instructor is in constant demand with beginning skiers. (Reyes photo)

FROM THE AUTHOR

My name is Larry Wild Wrice. After being a full time certified ski instructor for over 27 years – and after skiing all over the world for over fifty years, this method of teaching became my vision. My basic training, instruction method, and experience was acquired from the Vail Ski School in Colorado. During my many years as a student, instructor, and ski school director I became even more convinced that this book was a necessity. I have created these lessons using all of my knowledge, skills, and experience. After working many times with beginners, or as we would say "Never, Nevers," I know the method in this book will be of great help to anyone who wants to learn to ski or for those who want to improve their techniques.

After watching me instruct my students, a young man chose me to teach his girlfriend how to ski. He requested a one hour private session. Everything I told her to do, she did. I was impressed to see that she actually skied before the hour was over. After her lesson was over, he met me alone, and gave me a twenty dollar tip, saying "This is from the both of us. From the way you were teaching her, I learned more, myself, while watching from the sidelines, what I was doing wrong. You made me a better skier." He then asked me for one more private session. This time, he wanted me to ski along with her, and to correct her if necessary.

I bumped into him again, after her second lesson, and he stuck some money, again, in my hand, and repeated, "this is from the both of us." This time he had given me two twenty dollar bills. As he turned and walked away, the young man said something that I will always remember, "The reason why things were so private is because she is from the New York Ballet and because of her contract with them, I had to make sure she was in good hands and would not be injured." i appreciated his trust in me, but I also realized why, since she was a ballerina, she was able to learn so quickly. Dancers understand balance. Good body balance, and controlling your body weight, are the basics of good skiing. This book will teach you these, and many more important principles, that will help make you ready to ski.

7

BEGINNING TIPS

To be a good skier, you need to have good balance and correct weight distribution.

- Skiing is actually done on one foot.

- If you refer to the first lesson in this book where you learn a **WEDGE** turn there is your answer. No matter where you learn to ski, this wedge, formerly called a **SNOWPLOW** turn will be necessary to learn, as a beginning skier.

SKI WITH A FEELING

My motto for years has been, "Ski with a Feeling", which means two things:

- Learn to **FEEL** what your body is doing
- Learn how your body should **FEEL** when you are skiing.

The lessons in this book will place my motto in action, both in your living room and on the slopes.

- You will gain confidence and a much better understanding of what you are doing.
- These lessons will also assist and encourage you to get on the slopes and ski.

TABLE OF CONTENTS

DEDICATION

To John Sternbach, who started teaching at
Vail in 1964, at the same time that I did.
He is still my best friend

SIT DOWN IN YOUR CHAIR

AND

SKI WITH A FEELING!

1. FINDING YOUR FEET

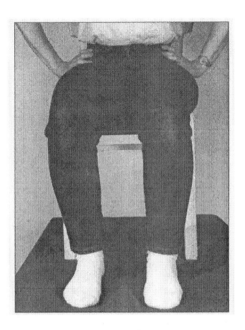

- Sit down on the edge of the chair, with your feet flat on the floor, about hip-width apart

- Now, roll both feet out, until you can feel the outside of your feet, with the arch of your feet up off the floor (see photo on following page)

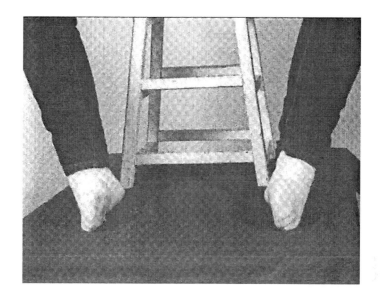

- Roll one foot in at a time, starting with your left foot. That means, bringing your left knee toward your right knee. You should feel your arch and your heel pressing on the floor. You should feel the outside of your left foot, in the air, off the floor.

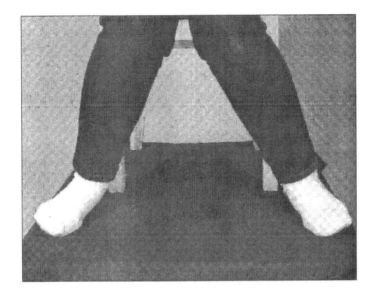

- Putting your left foot flat on the floor, do the same thing with your right knee and foot. Roll your right knee towards your left, feeling arch and heel pressing against the floor, and feeling the right side up off of the floor and in the air.

- Repeat these movements several times to get the understanding and feeling of the term "inside and outside

PLEASE NOTE:

You may notice that your knees are coming together.

THIS IS A NO NO! I repeat: a **NO NO!**

I will explain why in a later lesson

2. FINDING YOUR HEELS

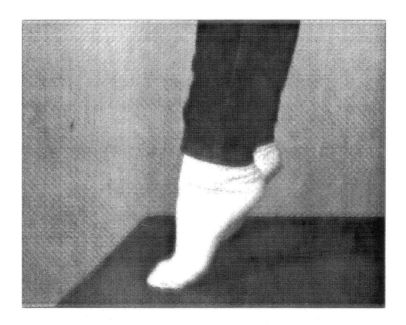

- Sitting on the edge of the chair, put your feet flat on the floor.

- Push your knees up in the air. Now you will find that your weight is on your toes,

- Drop your heels down. Now, you will find that your weight is on your heels.

- But we **DON'T** ski with our weight on our heels

3. FINDING THE BALLS OF YOUR FEET

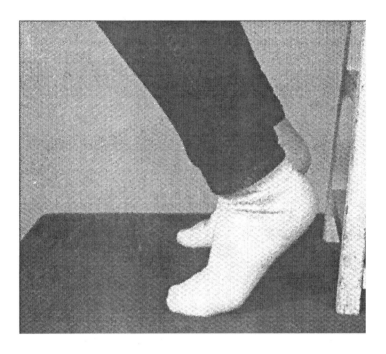

- Sit on the edge of your chair, with your feet flat on the floor

- Draw both feet back, until your heels are in the air.

- Remember, keep the weight on the balls of your feet

4. FINDING YOUR TOES

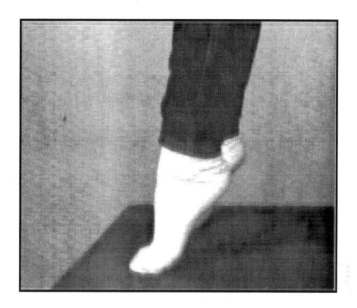

- Remain seated on the edge of your chair, with your feet flat on the floor

- Draw both feet back, until you feel your knees over your toes, and push both knees out. You will feel the weight on your little toes

- Now, roll both feet in, until the weight is on both big toes. You will notice that your knees are over your toes. This is very important, and will come up throughout this book. Knees forward **OVER** your toes. I must state again - this is very important

5. SITTING IN THE CHAIR

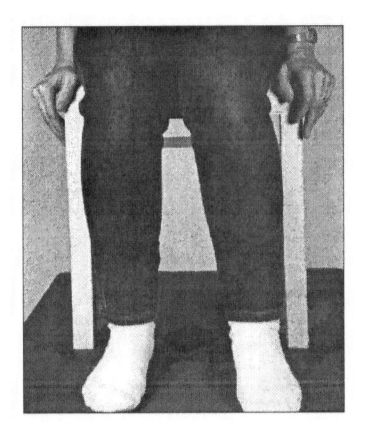

PLEASE NOTE:

Now, change your position on the chair. Move forward, putting both of the palms of your hands down on both sides of the chair. This will bring your knees over your toes.

6. SLIDING YOUR FEET

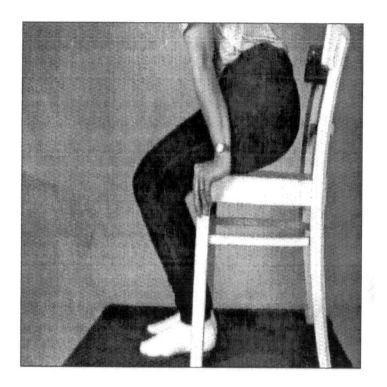

- Sit on the edge of your chair, with your palms down.

- Push down, with both hands, as if you were going to raise your body up out of the chair. While the pressure is on the palms of both hands, slide both feet back-and-forth.

- Then slide your feet, back and forth, one at a time

7. WALKING

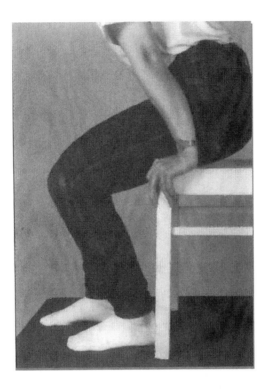

- Sitting on the edge of your chair, draw both feet back toward the chair. Leave both feet flat on the floor.

- Slide your right foot half a foot forward. While the weight is on the right foot slide your left foot half a foot forward. **THIS IS VERY IMPORTANT**: Before you move, bend your right knee forward over your right toe. Leave it there, adding weight to that foot before you move your left foot.

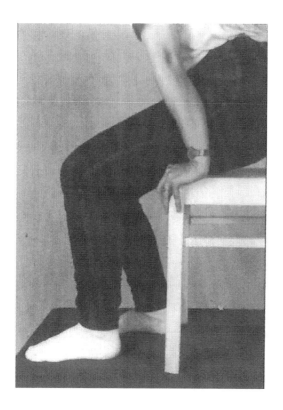

- NOW - Slide your left foot, half a foot forward, While the weight is on the left foot, slide your right foot, half a foot forward.

PLEASE NOTE: When walking in skis, your weight should **ALWAYS** be forward. You may be flat-footed in ski boots, but 85% of your weight should be on the balls of your feet, at all times.

- In other words, whatever you do on skis, from this point on, your WEIGHT MUST BE FORWARD. I repeat. Whatever you do, your weight must be forward. **PLEASE REMEMBER THIS**

8. CHANGING DIRECTIONS

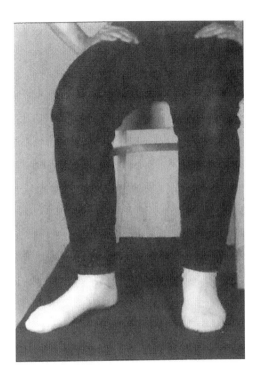

- Place the weight on the inside of the left foot, and then place the right foot half a foot to the right. Do this until you have completed a full circle. Never move your feet more than half a foot at a time.

- Even though, sitting in a chair, you may not be able to make a complete circle, move your feet as far as you can.

Again - Keep your knees bent and your weight **FORWARD**.

PLEASE NOTE:

- Now, turn, putting your weight on the inside of your left foot. Move your right foot half a foot. This means that your weight on your feet, (and later on your skis) is **FORWARD** and **DOWNHILL.**
- Now, move in the opposite direction, putting your weight on the inside of your right foot, in order to turn to your left. Turn your foot (ski) half a foot to the left.
- **AGAIN,** the weight will be on the **INSIDE** of the downhill foot, regardless of which way you turn. (This will be explained further in a later lesson)

9. PIVOTING

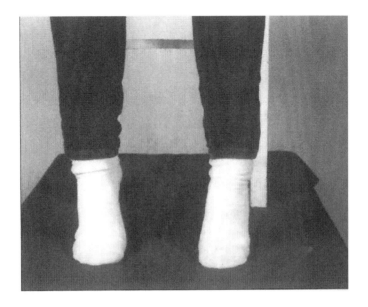

HERE IS HOW TO PIVOT:

- Sit on the edge of the chair, with your feet flat on the floor.

- Draw both feet back, toward the chair, again, until your heels are off the floor and your weight is on the balls of your feet.

- Turn both heels **OUT,** with the weight still on the balls of your feet. Then turn both heels **IN,** with the weight on the balls of your feet,

- Then turn your heels in and out **one at a time,**

- This is called **PIVOTING**

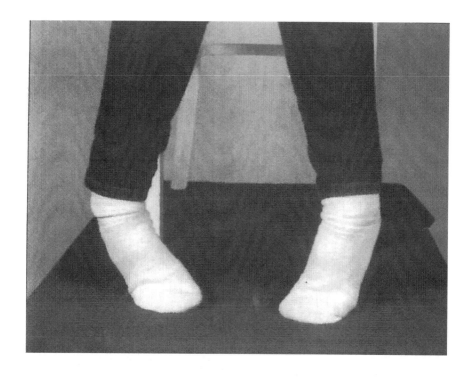

NOTE: STRAIGHT RUNNING

- Since this chapter contains movements done from a sitting position, my lesson on **STRAIGHT RUNNING**, is delayed until the following chapter.

- This essential movement teaches you to feel the skis under and alongside your body, and it must be done in a standing position. (**PLEASE NOTE**: your Straight Running lesson will be on page 48)

10. SLIDING HEELS IN AND OUT

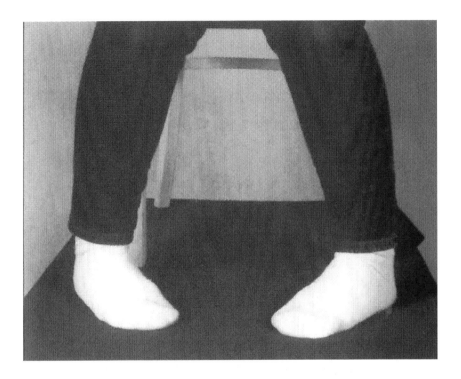

- Sit on the edge of the chair, with your feet flat on the floor. Slide both heels out, and slide both heels in.

- When you ski, slide your heels out, never in. To practice this: make sure that your ankles are slightly turned in, then, with your weight forward on the balls of your feet, slide your ankles in and out.

- This is what you will feel when you want to put your skis in a **WEDGE** stopping position

11. WEIGHT ON BIG TOES

- Put the palms of your hands down, on both sides of of the chair.

- Brace yourself, and slide both feet forward with the weight on each big toe. Your toes will be in and your heels will be out, just a little bit.

- Slide both feet forward, until your legs are almost straight

- Repeat this several times, until you gain the understanding and feeling. Remember, as this book states, you are learning to *SKI WITH A FEELING*

12. PIGEON TOED

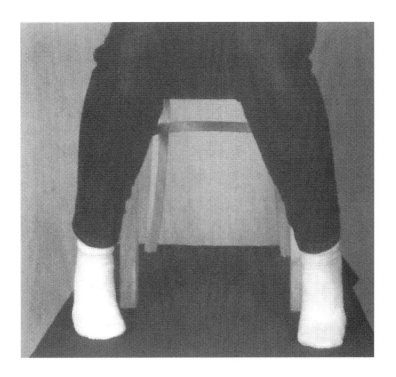

- Sit on the edge of the chair, palms down, on both sides. Now, let's slide both feet forward, with the pressure on the insides of your feet

- Now let's add pushing out on the heels.

- Repeat this, sliding your toes in, and your toes out. This is what we call **PIGEON-TOED.** Repeat this several times to gain understanding and more feeling. You are now learning to *SKI WITH A FEELING*

13. WEDGE

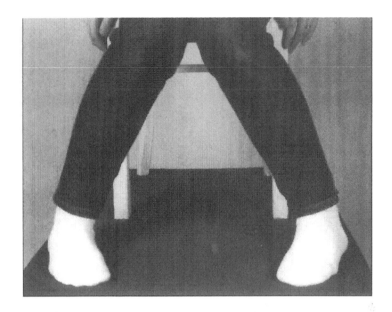

- The **WEDGE** is the second most essential movement after Straight Running. It is very important to know, so that you are able to control your speed and stop going down a hill.

- Sit on the chair with your feet flat on the floor in front of you. Step a half a foot to the side with the left foot and a half a foot to the side with the right foot. This will place both of your feet to the outside of your chair.

- Draw both feet back toward your chair. You will find the weight automatically goes to the balls of your feet. Make sure that your weight is on your big toes and your knees are forward over your toes. You will notice that your knees are not together – they should be about hip-width apart when you make your first run down the hill - in a **WEDGE**.

14. ROLLING ANKLES IN AND OUT.

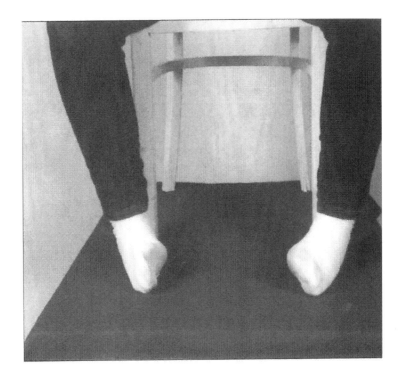

- In skiing, if you happen to be flat-footed, that is acceptable.

- However, if you let your ankles roll out - in other words, if you stand on the floor flat footed. and let your ankles roll out, to the extent that the inside of your feet are up – this is a **NO NO**

- When you practice, or when you ski on the snow, you **ALWAYS** want to stand with your knees forward and with your ankles rolled in. This is also called "standing on the **INSIDE OF YOUR FEET**"

15. SIDE - STEPPING

SIDE-STEPPING is the first method you need to know to walk up a hill. It is as essential as "straight running" and the "wedge." To learn this movement, sit on the edge of your chair, with your feet flat on the floor

Now roll both of your knees to the right to a point where the **INSIDE** of your left foot, and the **OUTSIDE** of your right foot, are on the floor

NOW, move your right foot up the hill. While doing this, **NEVER** move your foot over a half a foot at a time when going up

Repeat this uphill movement from side to side until you can get the feeling – and *SKI WITH A FEELING !*

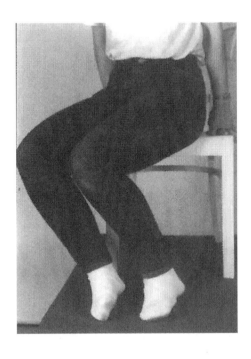

PART II

Now that you have learned various ski positions, while sitting on a chair, we will repeat everything you have learned, this time from a **STANDING POSITION**. This will simulate you actually standing on your skis. The movements of your feet will be identical to movements when you were sitting, and practicing them, while standing on your feet, will give you a better feeling.

- You will be standing using **TWO CHAIRS**.

- When standing on your feet let's make the **RIGHT SIDE UPHILL** and the **LEFT SIDE DOWNHILL**.

- To judge the hill from top to bottom, we will use count ONE to TEN. Number ONE (1) being the bottom of the hill, and Number TEN (10) being the top of the hill.

NOTE TO THE READER

To be successful on your first ski trip, it will help you greatly if you read and practice PART II and PART III of this book at least 3 or 4 times.

1. SKIING POSITION

This illustration shows the posture described below
as if you were holding a broom or mop handle

- Stand on both feet, back straight, feet about hip-width apart. Push both knees forward over your toes.

- Your heels should be **OFF** the floor about half an inch. Your hands should be forward, bent at the elbows, about hip high. **Example:** imagine your hands forward, as if you are carrying a tray in a cafeteria.

- **IMPORTANT:** Keep this position in mind, because having your hands forward is part of **BALANCE** and good posture, when you are skiing

2. STANDING BETWEEN TWO CHAIRS

Get two chairs with low backs. Put one chair on your left, and the other chair on your right

3. PLACEMENT OF HANDS ON CHAIRS

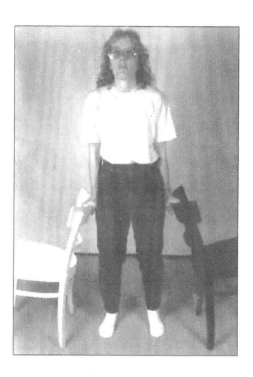

- If you are 5' 5" or under, your hands will be located on the sides of the chairs. If you are over 5' 5," then your hands will be placed on top of the chairs. The reason for this is: you must keep your arms straight and stiff at all times, never bending your elbows.

- When you are actually using your ski poles, your hands will always be located on the top of your poles, never down the sides. Also, try this with broomsticks

4. CHAIR POSITION

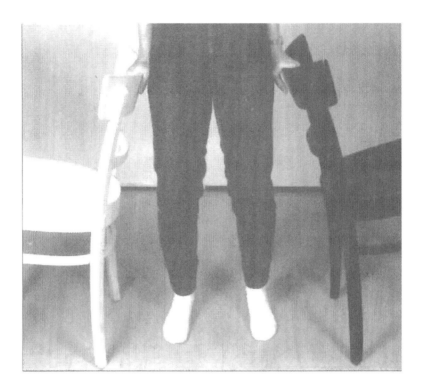

- Extend both chairs out, until the front chair legs are off the floor,

- Leave only the hind (back) legs of the chair on the floor.

- This position simulates the hind (back) legs of the chair being like ski poles, which, in this position, are an extension of your arms.

.5. BOUNCING

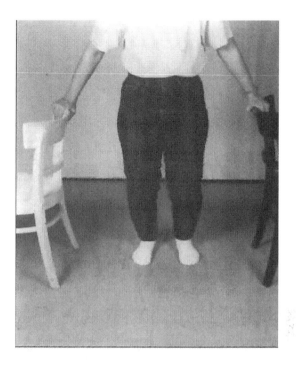

- Standing up, relaxed in your skiing position, start bouncing up and down. Each time you bounce, make sure that your knees are pushed forward.

- Do not drop your rear end behind your heels. Your rear end should come down above your heels, not behind them.

- Make sure when bouncing, that your weight stays on the inside of your feet and over your big toes.

- The magic word now is **RELAX**. Repeat this until you understand and feel - and *SKI WITH A FEELING!*

6. SLIDING YOUR FEET

- You have already done this exercise seated in a chair.

- NOW brace yourself, on both chairs, in a standing position

- Standing up, between two chairs, slide both feet back and forth

- Then slide each foot back and forth, one at a time.
(This movement was shown seated in Part I Lesson 6)

7. CHANGING DIRECTIONS

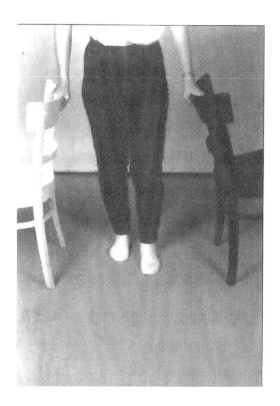

- Still standing between two chairs, first start toward your left. Put your weight on the inside of your right foot; then step to the left, half a foot.

- Now, bring your right foot next to your left foot. Repeat this movement, until you can go all the way around in a circle. Do this as far as you can, in a standing position.

- Now, do the same exercise to the right side, and remember, this time, to have your weight on the inside of your left foot

8. WALKING

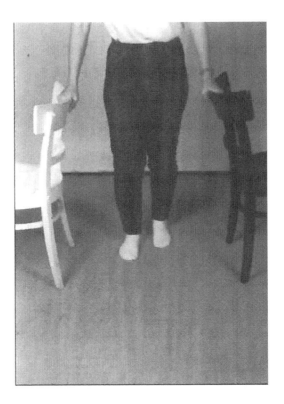

- Standing between your chairs, slide your left foot forward about a foot. Bending your knee, put your weight on your left foot

- Now, while the weight is there, slide your right foot, forward, about a foot. This time, bend that knee and put the weight on your right foot.

- Notice that your weight is always forward, when you slide your foot ahead

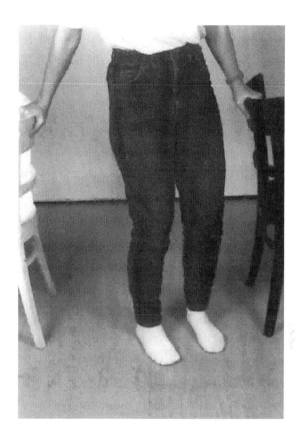

NOTE: When walking with ski poles, your hands are placed on the top of the poles.
When placing the poles on the ground, make sure the tips of the poles are **ALWAYS** behind your heels.

9. SIDE-STEPPING

- Place your hands on both chairs. Keep your arms straight and stiff, and don't bend your elbows.

- Push both knees forward over your toes. Push both knees to the right. Move your right foot up the hill half a foot.

- Move your left foot up to your right foot. Whenever you put your right foot down, make sure your weight is on the **OUTSIDE** of your **RIGHT** foot . Whenever you put your left foot down, make sure the weight is on the **INSIDE** of your **LEFT** foot

Never put your foot down flat when you're doing this exercise. Repeat this exercise several times, on both the left side, and the right side.

Remember, whenever you do SIDE-STEPPING, you always move your uphill foot first, with the weight on the inside of your downhill foot. This is the way you will move uphill when the hill is too steep to walk straight up

Repeat this exercise several times until you understand it and you feel it ... which is what we call

Ski with a Feeling !

10. GETTING READY TO TURN

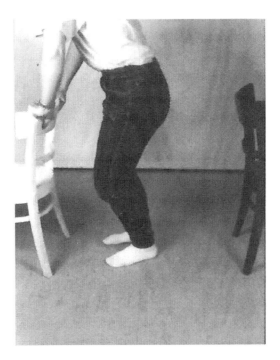

- After sidestepping up the hill, you will want to learn to turn, and come down the hill

- To start a turn, place both poles down the hill at an angle. This will stop you from sliding downhill before you complete your turn. Now, place both hands on top of the poles and place your weight on top of your poles. Step back, with the right foot, a half a foot backward, this followed by your left foot. Continue this until both feet are facing downhill.

- While doing this exercise, keep both arms straight, never bending your elbows

NOTE ON SKI POLES: When using poles, turn at the waist, with the palms of your hands on top of your poles. Place the poles two feet in front of your toes, at an angle, where 85% of your weight is on the poles.

This section of the book is about

LEARNING TO TURN

NOTE TO THE READER:

To be successful on your first ski trip, it will help you greatly to read and practice PART II and PART III of this book at least three or four times

1. MAKING YOUR FIRST DOWNHILL RUN

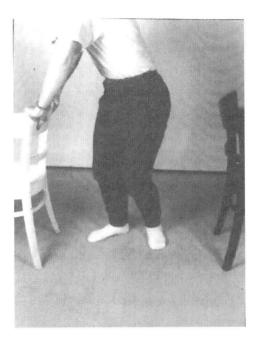

- Place the palms of your hands on the top of one chair. The back legs of the chair will simulate ski poles

- To get both feet behind your chair (ski poles), step back, turning your right foot ¼ of a turn in. Bring your left foot back to the right. Repeat, with the right foot again. This will bring your right toe pointed behind the chair (facing downhill). Now, bring the left foot next to the right. Both toes will now be behind the chair (ski poles).

- This exercise will prevent you from crossing your skis while making a downhill turn.**REMEMBER:** When you move the right foot out, keep your weight on the inside of your left foot at all times. When you are moving your right foot back, the rest of your weight will be on the back of the chair (ski poles)

2. STRAIGHT RUNNING

- After you have made your first turn, you will be in a position for STRAIGHT RUNNING, using both of your chairs to simulate ski poles. (NOTE: Straight running can be practiced, with or without poles, but using the chairs can give you a more clear understanding of how this movement should look and feel)

- Stand with your poles at an angle, with the palms of your hands on top of the poles, about a hip-width apart. Release your weight from the poles by pushing both arms forward. When you are on skis, this will cause you to slide on your skis down the hill. Both knees should be pushed forward, over your toes. Your back should be straight, with a little weight on the inside of both of your feet

- As you pass downhill, between your poles, imagine picking your poles up and holding them in the air. Remember, sliding down the hill, your feet should be a hip-width apart.

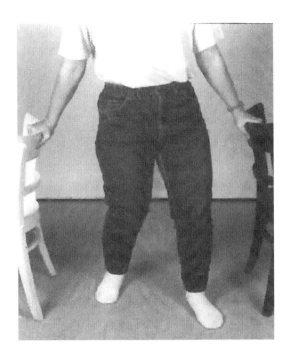

NOTE: After you have mastered this, **SIDE-STEP** up the hill 10 feet. Then try 20 feet. Again, repeat from both sides. As you will notice, you will have walked all the way around until your toes are pointed back up the hill

At the bottom of the run, step out with your right foot a half a foot, left foot following until skies are pointed uphill

3. SLIDING FEET OUT IN PLASTIC BAGS

IMPORTANT NOTE: The use of plastic bags is **OPTIONAL,** and, should be done, only, with someone providing assistance and support to you, if necessary, to protect you from slipping or falling

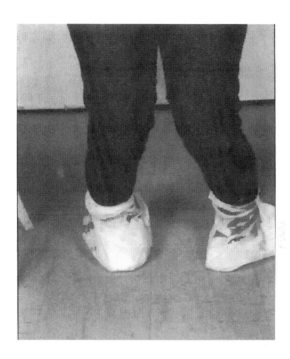

- **OPTIONAL:** Put plastic bags over your socks.

- Stand behind your chair, holding it firmly, with your feet a hip-width apart, and the palms of your hands on the back of your chair.

- Push both knees forward, over your toes. Put the weight over the big toe and slide both heels out which will bring your feet into a wedge position. Practice this until you understand and get the feeling

4. WEDGE IN PLASTIC BAGS

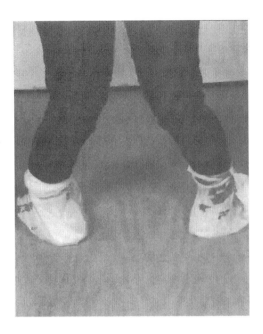

- The next important thing in skiing is how to stop or control your speed coming down a hill.. ***Take your time, concentrate and learn this well.***

- We have already done this WEDGE exercise sitting on the edge of a chair. Now, you will practice it, in a standing position.

- To get the authentic feeling, you will need to practice this on a smooth floor or on a piece of masonite or very stiff cardboard 4 x 4 feet.

NOTE: Again, please note that the above movement should be done, only, with someone providing assistance and support to you, if necessary, to protect you from slipping or falling

UP AND DOWN THE HILL

- In order to practice the **WEDGE,** you must first side-step up the hill, starting at the bottom with a 1 count and going all the way up to the 10 count, which simulates that you have reached the top of the hill.

- Now, make your turn at the waist only, placing both poles down the hill at an angle. Keep the palms of your hands on top of your poles, and keep your arms straight and stiff.

- Bring your feet behind your poles. Now, put your feet in a wedge position and start sliding down the hill, again counting from 10 to 1. This time #1 is simulating that you have reached the bottom of the hill.

- On the snow, you would do the same thing, and you would do it as slowly as you can.

- Repeat this movement, until you are comfortable with it , and have the feeling that you can stop when **YOU** want to.

5. STEP TURNS

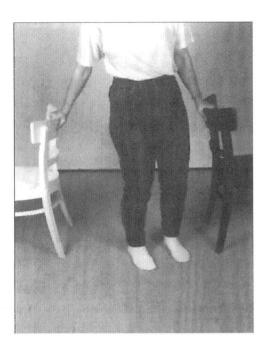

- When you are at the bottom of the hill, put your weight on the inside of your right foot

- Step to the left, half a foot away. Repeat this until both feet are pointed back up the hill

- Now, side step back up the hill and make your turn.

- Then, come back down the hill again. This time, put your weight on the inside of your left foot. Step to the right, and repeat this movement until both feet are pointed up the hill.

- Repeat on both sides until you are comfortable and can feel it - FEEL IT – AND **SKI WITH A FEELING !**

6. LEARNING TO TURN

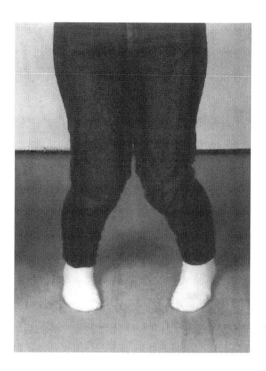

LEARNING TO TURN is one of the most important parts of your skiing career. It is a double must that this next exercise becomes a part of you, It should become just as easy as walking down the street, while not even thinking about it. In other words, the turning movement should become second nature to you. Let's start!

- Put your feet in your pigeon-toed position. Your feet should be about shoulder-width apart, with your knees pushed forward over your toes.

- It is extremely important in this exercise to keep your weight on the **INSIDE** of your **DOWNHILL** foot. 85% of your weight should be on the balls of your feet and your big toe throughout your turn

7. EXAGGERATED TURNING POSITION

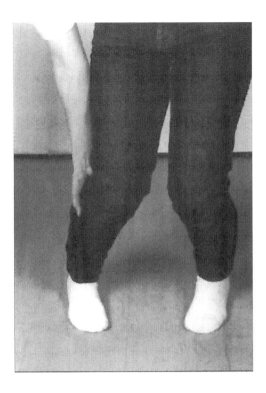

- Start down the hill, in your wedge position

- Now - reach down with your right hand, and grab your right calf.

- Keep your knees bent and your weight forward. Now, all of your weight should be on the inside of your right foot.

- Hold this position until your right foot turns "into the hill."

- Repeat this movement, now, on your left side

8. TURNING WITH SHOULDER POSITION

- Start down the hill, in your wedge, with your hands on your hips. Push your left hand into your side, and drop your left shoulder back a little, over the side of your left hip. Now, push your left knee forward, over your left big toe, pressing on your big toe. Hold that position, until your left foot is pointed back "into the hill."

- Do the same thing on your right side. Push your right hand into your side, drop your right shoulder a little back over your right hip. Push your right knee over your right big toe, pressing down. Hold this position until your right foot is pointed " into the hill."

   REMEMBER: Your hips should stay between your skis and your feet to do this exercise correctly.

9. TURNING / WEIGHT TRANSFER

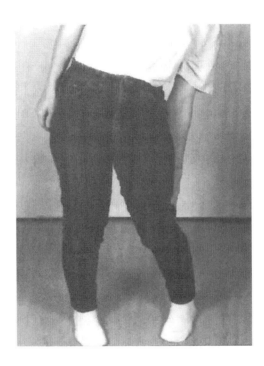

- In order to control your skis going down the hill, you must always have your weight in the proper place, on the skis. Please remember this.

- To control your speed during the turn – it is also **ESSENTIAL** that your weight is in the proper place.

- For perfect control of your turns, keep your weight forward and on the inside of your downhill foot. Changing weight, from the inside of your left foot to the inside of your right foot, is called **WEIGHT TRANSFER.**

NOTE:

HOW TO PARALLEL SKI

- The art of skiing for each individual – or the HEIGHT of skiing is to **PARALLEL SKI**

- In order to parallel ski, you must turn, with all of your weight, on the inside of your foot – may it be left or right - as long as it is your **DOWNHILL SKI.**

- If you maintain the majority of your weight on the inside - left or right -- when you are turning,   the opposite ski will follow in its path. Master this and that is when you become a **PARALLEL SKIER**

PART IV

In this section of the book, you will learn about clothing and rental equipment

CLOTHING

LET'S START FROM THE INSIDE OUT!

LOWER BODY WEAR: Make sure that you have thermal underwear on top and bottom. There are all types of thermal underwear and they all work; it is really a matter of how much you want to spend. The ladies have an advantage over the guys - women often have in their wardrobe, pantyhose that can give their legs double insulation I would advise the guys to wear the same, but when a man pulls his pants down, some people may not understand. Speaking now of undergarments, something else is available on the market! Don't quote me on this but some people are wearing thermal underwear and also wearing bike knee pants over the top of the thermal underwear for double insulation. It is all really your choice. Here is another personal suggestion: I do not recommend jeans for several reasons. the main reason is that they are not water resistant, not even with Scotchguard. Find something to wear that is warm and comfortable and water resistant. Check out the department stores, discount stores, sports outlet stores, for what is called "bib" ski pants. These do not need to be expensive to be effective

UPPER BODY WEAR: The next thing you will need is something warm on top of your thermal underwear. A nice cotton turtleneck, a thermal turtleneck, or a slipover sweater of some kind is good. The reason for this, believe it or not, even in the cold weather, while learning to ski, you will sweat heavily. In order not to catch cold, a plastic shirt or jumper will keep the cold out and the moisture in. A nice plastic shirt would be next with a nice warm wool sweater. Follow that with a nice warm jacket, preferably a waterproof one

HANDS AND FEET : The next two areas to concentrate on are your hands and feet. No one has come up with a sure guarantee that their product will keep your hands and feet from getting cold. However, let's start with your hands. My personal advice is: don't go to the ski area with the gloves and scarf combination that Grandma may have knitted for you last Christmas. Most likely, they won't work effectively. The best thing to wear are mittens. Keeping your fingers close together will also help to keep them warm, so find ski gloves that will do that. There are a wide ranges of prices to choose from. Do not purchase the cheap nylon ones because there are good gloves that are reasonably priced.

Now for your feet, I personally recommend wool socks. Wool socks that have good padding. My own advice is to wear only one pair of socks. Some people prefer wearing two, but one pair should be all that is necessary, Too many pairs of socks will give you the wrong fitting in your boots.

HEADWEAR, EARS AND EYE PROTECTION: Let's not forget about our head and ears. Science says that heat loss is from the top of the head, so be sure to find yourself a nice wool hat for your head, which you can pull down over your ears. Another very important item is something to cover your eyes. I don't say you need to go out and buy expensive ski goggles, but I do say to find a good, strong pair of sunglasses to put over your eyes while you are skiing. The reflection of the sun on the snow can give you eye poisoning; this is a serious condition and can cause your eyes to swell closed. I hope that you take this advice seriously.

BOOTS

The next area of importance is your boots. Skis and poles can come later. Be sure you buy a good pair of boots. They are expensive and should be well fitted to provide you with years of enjoyment. If you are hesitating to purchase expensive equipment at this time, be certain first that this is a sport you plan to pursue. There are many reputable rental shops in the ski areas to help you get started. If you go to a rental shop, ask for boots that are the same size as the shoes you wear. When you stick your foot into the boot, it will seem strange to you. This is natural; they are heavy and awkward and clumsy

For a comfortable boot, I recommend a rear entry boot. The boot must be firm under the arch. It should also be loose enough in the toes, once you buckle it up, that you can wiggle all of your toes and feel them. Once the boots are buckled, push your knees forward over the tops of your boots and wiggle your toes to be sure they are free. If the heel comes up in the back of the boot about a quarter of an inch that is not an ill-fitted boot - that is normal. Once you are satisfied with the fit and you are leaving the rental shop, go to the hill, unbuckle your top buckle so that you can walk easily in your boots. The way to walk is always to put the heel down first, then the toe.

NOTE: to make sure you have a good fitted boot when you are walking, you will find your toes right against the front of the boot. You might at first think that your boots are too small, but buckle them up first, and bend or push both knees forward. Then, notice, by pushing forward, if there is no pressure on your toes. That is the way to check for proper fit

Do not purchase any equipment at this time. First, be certain that this is a sport that you plan to pursue. There are many reputable rental shops in the ski areas to help you get started. When you get skis for the first day you are on the hill, you should have skis that are a size 150, unless you are 6 feet tall or more and weigh over 150 pounds. If you fit into that category, then you should ask for a size 165. As a rule, size 150 is the shortest (adult) ski available and all beginners should use this size; it is easier to handle and easier to maneuver

Ski poles are to be judged by merely bending both elbows to a point that it looks as if you are carrying a tray in the cafeteria Turn your ski poles upside down, so that the handles are resting on the ground and that the tips are up. Wrap all four fingers around the tips, so that your hands are resting on the basket. Remember, your forearms should be parallel to the ground

. WHAT A SKI WILL DO

- If a ski is flat, and you point it downhill, it is going to go straight down the hill. If it hits a bump , it may turn. If it runs into any object, it will change its path.

- It goes back to what I said in the beginning of the book. Your balance and weight transfer or weight distribution, will determine which way a ski will go.

- But you must remember this. Consider one ski with 85 percent of your weight and the other ski with only 15 percent of your weight. The ski that has most weight, will turn in the direction that you want to go.

- All you have to think of then, is the principle similar to the principle used when someone is surfing, skateboarding or snow-boarding, You lean forward toward the direction you want to

- go. But skiing becomes a one foot operation and therefore, you have to think only of one ski, as if thinking of only one snowboard.

- Here's the trick. If you lean too far on your turn, you will fall. So what you are trying to do is to balance yourself on that edge of the ski, snowboard, or slalom that is holding you up.

- REMEMBER: When turning, the weight is **ALWAYS** on the **INSIDE (DOWNHILL) SKI.**

- If you practice correct wedge turns, you will gain the necessary confidence that you will need to control your skis.

PERSONAL TIPS

- To have a better chance of avoiding an accident as a beginning skier **NEVER** stick ski poles in front of you in the snow to stop going downhill

- When walking with your ski poles, keep your weight forward, and the tips of your poles always behind your heels, with the palms of your hands on top of your ski poles.

- You do not ski with the muscles of your body. Instead, you learn to relax, standing on the skeleton of the body, using your natural weight to control your skis, not your muscles.

REMEMBER: SO THAT YOU ARE PREPARED TO BE MORE SUCCESSFUL ON YOUR FIRST SKI TRIP, READ PART TWO AND THREE OF THIS BOOK AND PRACTICE THE LESSSONS AT LEAST THREE OR FOUR TIMES

ABOUT THE AUTHOR

Larry 'Wild' Wrice is a man with many talents. He was born on the south side of the windy city of Chicago, Illinois. There, he first started dancing with Sadie Bruce and began playing drums at the George L Giles American Legion Post. Larry furthered his drumming career at the Willard Theater on 51st Street in Chicago. His very successful musical career as a double bass drummer and a band leader was first launched and then continued all over the world from there.

Larry's second 27 year career as a very popular professional ski instructor led to the creation of this book, SKI IN YOUR STOCKING FEET, an updated edition of his popular 1986 edition. Larry's additional expertise in the area of fitness and longevity also led to the publication of his second book, 28 STEPS TO LIFE – a groundbreaking method of movements that are all done, while lying in bed, before your feet hit the floor in the morning. This book, and Larry's other publications can be purchased at this E Store website which is:

https://www.createspace.com/4266003

MORE ABOUT THE AUTHOR

26

JOHNNY REYES RAPPING ON
NEWS FROM AROUND THE SKIING WORLD

Chicago Daily Defender February 3, 1973

One of Playboy's assets, is the presence of Larry Wrice, a black Associate Ski Instructor, who is one of the more popular instructors at the area. Called, "Wild Rice" by many, Larry started skiing 7 years ago, and held his first job at Vail, Colorado, then moved on for a year at Hunter's Mountain, in the East. Since coming to Playboy in 1967, Wrice is constantly in demand and on the average, instructs about 100 skiers per week, of which 85 percent returns for more advanced lessons.

One of 6 black instructors who is active in the PSIA (Professional Ski Instructors of America, Wrice hopes to achieve his full certification this year. Because of heavy demands on his teaching time, he hopes to get out more often, to be able to pass the Free Skiing stage of the PSIA test. Larry is also an accomplished musician, and has backed up such recording stars as Dinah Washington, Ella Fitzgerald, Nancy Wilson, and has been a studio drummer for Motown.

33943389R00040

Printed in Poland
by Amazon Fulfillment
Poland Sp. z o.o., Wrocław